Jonathan Steffen .

THE COLOUR OF LOVE

JONATHAN STEFFEN

ACUMEN PUBLICATIONS

2011

ACKNOWLEDGEMENTS are due to the following: *'Studio', 'Autumn Scene', 'Lavender', 'Kipper Tie' and 'Heidelberg' were first published in* Poetic Pilgrimages: James Hogg at Eighty *(ed. Wolfgang Görtschacher and Andreas Schachermayr. Salzburg, 2011.) 'Apprentice and Master' was first published in* Acumen Literary Journal

British Library C-i-P data:
A catalogue record for this pamphlet is available from the British Library.

ISBN: 978 - 1 - 873161 - 32 - 6

Published by
ACUMEN PUBLICATIONS
6 The Mount
Higher Furzeham
Brixham
South Devon
TQ5 8QY
UK

Printed by
AC Print, Higher Furzeham, Brixham, Devon.

CONTENTS

To everyone who can be
a rainbow to someone else;
and to someone who was
a rainbow for me in a
dark hour.

The Colour of Love

Please let us try to forgive one another.
I shall forgive you your Rose Madder moments,
Your Prussian Blue moods
And your Vandyke Brown studies
If you will forgive me my Scarlet Lake,
My all-too-Transparent Maroon,
And, of course, my Viridian.
I accept your Quinacridone Magenta,
Although I have difficulty pronouncing it,
Your ominously named Mauve Blue Shade,
And even your perplexing Ivory Black (!?!).
Please leave me alone with my Permanent Green
(It is *permanent*),
My Cadmium Scarlet (can't get enough scarlet!)
And my Phthalo Turquoise.
I don't care if you think it's pretentious.
Please let us try to forgive one another.
I know no word for the colour of love.

The Colours of My Heart

I know the colours of my heart:
The green of hope that cannot die,
The red of blood that cannot lie,
The white, a sacred space for art.
They form the prayer flag of my mind:
A dancing green, a pulsing red,
A white that shows what can't be said.
They paint my private skies, and wind
Themselves – one here, one there –
Like ribbons, softly, in your hair.

For You in Sleep

You are sleeping as I write these lines,
Hundreds of miles away from me.
I do not know the colour of your sheets.
I do not know the colour of your nightdress.
I do not know the colour of your dreams.
But I am sending you
My deepest greens and softest blues,
Serene and soothing oceanic colours,
For you to safely drift on, my love,
As you make your gradual way towards another day.

Rainbow

I have never told you,
But I collect rainbows for you
As I make my way through the world.
They are easy to find;
I see them everywhere I go, in fact.
For instance, the red of the neon sign
Of this hotel's name
Reflected in a Rotterdam canal
An hour before sunrise.
The orange of a bottle
Of complimentary shower gel,
Evoking Spanish courtyards,
Relaxation tapes,
Corporate hotels with complimentary shower
gel ...
The yellow of a sachet of chamomile tea,
Chosen in preference to coffee
During yet another insufficiently long coffee break
At this interminable conference
(Drunk enough coffee already today).
The green of half a kiwi fruit in its skin
Which I simply *cannot deal with*
Whilst attempting to appear involved
In multiple simultaneous conversations over lunch.
The blue of the tenth PowerPoint template
I have seen today
Whose predominant colour is blue.
The indigo of the four-in-the afternoon sky,
Glimpsed briefly and freezingly
Between skyscrapers and breakout sessions.

The violet of a bizarrely coloured mint
That has been positioned
On the duvet of my hotel bed
To make me feel fractionally less alone tonight.
Yes, I collect rainbows when I am out and about.
It comes very naturally to me.
Here is another one for you.

Forbidden Fruit

Cherry and apricot,
Kiwi and pineapple:
What an extraordinarily
Attractive shawl
You are wearing,
If I may make so bold.

Kipper Tie

It was tangerine orange and chocolate brown,
Turquoise blue and mustard yellow,
Cerise pink and lime green.
Those were the colours of the early 'seventies –
A world of suburban psychadelia
In which we lived behind tangerine front doors
And lolled around on chocolate sofas,
Wore turquoise hot pants and mustard flares,
Sported cerise button-downs and lime bikinis.
It was the world of Kodachrome and Polaroid,
Of colour TV and colour supplements,
Of album covers that looked like mandalas,
And mandalas that looked like album covers,
And kipper ties that looked like everything on earth.
And, over and over again,
We captured ourselves on Agfacolor and FujiFilm,
Squeezing the vivid spectrum of our existences
Into snap upon snap upon snap
Shot in our sun-filled back gardens
And around our crowded coffee tables,
Little imagining that within our own brief lifetimes
Our beloved colour photographs would fade
And all our youth dissolve
Into a gradually receding blur.

Manitas de Plata

Lamp Black, Pewter and Zinc
Create the colours of my childhood.
Grainy and flickering,
Sliding and intermittent,
They depict the assassination of JFK
And the funeral of Churchill,
The first triumphs of the Beatles
And the first defeats of the Vietnam War,
Bobby Moore eternally holding the World Cup
                                        aloft
And Gene Pitney endlessly caught 24 hours
                                        from Tulsa.
Twiggy and Mao Tse Tung were black and white.
Christine Keeler was black and white.
Even Segovia was black and white.
But Manitas de Plata played in colour,
The blood reds and arena yellows,
The flick-knife silvers and bougainvillea violets,
The midnight blues and the hot flesh pinks
Of his percussive, rippling flamenco guitar
Pouring into my monochrome world
With all the measureless grace
Of a matador's tossed cape.

The Colour of Your Skin

What was the colour of your mother's favourite
                                    dressing-gown?
Or your father's favourite cardigan?
What was the colour of your first front door?
Or your first bicycle?
Or your first party dress?
And what, I wonder,
Was the colour of your first heartbreak ...?
I know so little of you;
I sense so much.
I know the colour of your eyes.
I know the colour of your hair.
And I can sense the colour of your skin,
My well-known stranger,
Where you can't even see it.

Colouring by Numbers

Now, listen to me.
I have thought long and hard
About the colour of your hair.
And I have thought long and hard
About the colour of your eyes.
But what interests me right now
Is the colour of the hairs on your forearms –
The mystically indescribable colouring of the hairs
On your inexpressibly beautiful forearms.
I may perhaps never be able
To name that colour.
But I could, if you were willing,
Count the hairs on your forearms.
Which would take me,
I am pleased to reflect,
An unconscionably long time.
I am ready to start this instant.

Bedroom Orange

A wiser man than me –
A finer heart, a better lover –
Might exercise restraint
And choose a softer palette for your praise.
He might, in all his self-command,
Paint you in subtly muted tones –
In pastel blues that are almost green,
In watercolour reds that are almost brown.
He might even have the self-denial
To eschew all colour
And depict you in charcoal, or pencil, or ink.
He might leave a lot of white space for the
                                        imagination.
He might delicately adumbrate the possibility
Of ever understanding any aspect of you
With a few well-chosen lines
Of discreet monochrome.
I am not that man, however,
And I never could be.
And so I want to paint you
In colours that haven't been invented yet:
Nostalgia green,
Pulse red,
Disclosure white,
Against-all-odds yellow,
Total commitment blue,
Forgiveness purple,
Bedroom orange.
I have no idea what it means –
I have absolutely no idea what it means –

But yes,
I would certainly need to use
Quantities of bedroom orange.

Home-making

At First Dawn™, it was Timeless™:
They wanted to enjoy the same Crazy Cream™
On the same Distant Shore™.
But it proved to be an Illusion™.
He wanted Sexy Pink™, Roasted Red™,
And, at least, a touch of Raspberry Diva™.
She wanted Sugared Lilac™, Soft Vanilla,
And, at most, a little Nude Glow™.
He wanted them to go to the Wild Forest™.
She wanted them to go to the Nordic Spa™.
He looked for Intense Truffle™;
He encountered Dusted Fondant™.
And so the first Ocean Ripple™ came.
Whipped up by a Desert Wind™,
It grew inevitably into a Sea Storm™.
When that subsided, all that was left
Was an Atmosphere™ of Frosted Steel™ –
And, whoever's fault it may or may not have been,
The same Blue Reflection™.

Recovery Room

There is no need to describe the pain you are in.
It speaks in every look and gesture.
Listen.
I have Flake White for you,
As much Flake White as you need.
I shall make bandages,
Soft, white bandages
To wrap and bind and hold you.
I shall put you in the stillest and whitest of beds.
I shall place that bed in the stillest and whitest
                                          of rooms
With a high, clean ceiling.
Then I shall take Cadmium Yellow,
Chrome Yellow and Cadmium Green,
And at the foot of your bed
I shall place a spray of daffodils.
Look at daffodils: they are enough for now.
Pray for some sunshine
Through the high window I have given you.

The Colour of Grief

I do not think that there is a colour for grief.
No black or grey,
No icy blue or putrid green or acid yellow
Could express the feeling.
It is like having ashes in your mouth
And gravel in the skin of your palms.
It is like weeping with every pore of your body.
It is like freezing all the way
From the centre of your heart
To the furthest edges of the universe.
Grief has no measure, no shape, and no horizon.
Perhaps only an artist
Who could create a colour that is beyond all colour
Could depict the colour of grief.

Hotdesking Room

It is the colour of indifference,
The colour of neglect,
The colour of corporate write-offs.
These greys and creams and beiges
Must once have had names.
Monday Tone.
Briefing Hue.
Matt Workflow.
The light of unrelenting commercial skies
Filters through paralytic blinds
To enter into an arm's-length relationship
With gummy keyboards and fading flatscreens,
With empty coffee-cups and wilting Post-It notes,
And *that poor office plant* ...
And this, my darling,
Is the room where I first saw you,
And your aura still hangs,
Like a miraculously misplaced rainbow,
On the recycled office air.

Primary Colours

I miss you
As yellow misses purple,
As blue misses orange,
As red misses green.
And if there were
Another primary colour,
I would miss you
In another way.

Rosemary

Quintessentially reproducible,
As true as a Pantone number,
You appear
On my steak,
In my bath,
In my Homer;
Stupendously self-reliant
And eternally neglected;
Herb of the gods.

Autumn Scene

I cannot paint the colours of this autumn scene,
But I can help you paint them for yourself, if you
                                                  will.
Think of the tenderest hopes to which you still
                                                  cling.
Think of your moment of profoundest serenity.
Think of the passions that burn within you still.
Think of your deepest and most enduring loss.
Then think, if you will,
Of the fear of being torn from your home,
And crumpled up, and thrown aside,
And trampled underfoot, and left to rot where
                                                  you fall.
– Yes indeed, that is the winter wind you feel
                                                  blowing.

Winter Landscape

Hard to describe the colours of this winter landscape.
They are bleached by the milky veil of freezing air
And anyway, it is so cold one can barely think.
But if I strive, I can discern
Thin russets and dull olives and gun-metal greys
Among the naked trees;
I can see how the snow on the hilltops
Is tinged with pale blue
And the snow by the roadsides
Is tinged with khaki.
Here and there a patch of bracken
Huddles in the blankness like a group of shaggy ponies.
Three crows perch on the top of an oak tree,
The only true black in the scene.
And the sky …
The sky is a colour that hovers between grey and white,
The colour of the promise of more snow to come.
From the colour, I cannot say when it will come.
Nor can I say when I will see you again.
But this is a winter scene,
And the light is already starting to fade,
And it is far too cold for any more words now.

It was the deepest, darkest point of the year ...

It was the deepest, darkest point of the year. I drove south to Italy, south towards the light. I arrived in pitch blackness on Christmas Eve.

Leaving the highway, I drove towards the lakeside on roads that became ever more winding, and rutted, and ancient. Eventually I had to park the car and thread my way down to the water's edge on foot. It was so dark that it was impossible to make out the buildings on either side of the narrow, cobbled lanes. I walked and walked, hesitantly, my hand outstretched before me like a blind man's.

Suddenly I stepped into a cloud of incense. It was emanating from the open door of a church where Mass must just have been celebrated. Breathing in the smoky, multi-layered scent, I was transported back two thousand years, caught in the vision of a vanished, never-lost world. I saw the gold of earrings and the silver of bracelets, the copper of goblets and the iron of spearheads, the crimson of pomegranates and the purple of figs, the green of olives and the yellow of saffron, the blue of lapis lazuli and the grey of ambergris, the pink of rosewater and the cream of unleavened bread, the brown of breastplates and the beige of wineskins, the black of nails and the white of bandages.

And yes, I saw the indigo of a night sky. And yes, I saw the shining of a star with no answers. And yes, of course, at last, at last I had to see the red of the blood of Christ.

Austria

Oh, do not change, I beg you, do not change:
I need your greens and blues to stay the same,
The loved and long-familiar colour range
That in my heart can only have one name.
My Austria, my Austria – you are
The distant forest green of deepest rest,
The sapphire of a lake seen from afar,
The red of quietly sleeping rooftops blessed
By centuries of slowly tolling bells.
You are the dancing white of sunwashed walls,
The burgeoning vermilion wave that wells
Over ten million balconies and falls
Right in the middle of the stranger's soul.
You are the mountains of my inner peace,
The streams that flow as one to make me whole,
The longed-for homeland of a lifetime's lease.
Oh, do not change, I beg you, stay the same:
Even the wanderer may stake this claim.

Heidelberg

You have so many colours,
My Heidelberg,
My borrowed patch of home,
And I can see them all, as unchanged
As if I felt your cobbles still beneath my feet.
I see the Chrome Green of your wooded hillsides,
The hillscape of your rooftops,
Cadmium Scarlet rubbing shoulders with Blue Black;
I see the Jesuit harmonies
Of Alzarin Crimson, Naples Yellow and Zinc White
Plunged deep within your Protestant soul.
And then your springtime trees in blossom:
Iridescent White for the almonds, the first to flower,
Rose Madder for the cherries,
Permanent Carmine for the plums ...
But if I had to choose a single colour for you,
You long-lost capital of a vanished land,
It could only be your red sandstone,
The Terra Rosa of your castle built on sand,
Glowing in the long, long, valley light,
Adored and adorned and then blown apart,
Like a heritage, a home,
A family, a heart.

Unter den Linden

How do you paint the colours of a breeze?
I have no names, and yet I feel it on my face
As palpable as if it were still May 1982
And we were sitting in that street café
Unter den Linden, in East Berlin:
Warm-cool, quick-slow, here and there and here
                                        again,
Tugging at our faces just as love was tugging at
                                        our hearts.
I can tell you the colour of the linden trees:
Permanent Green Light.
(It has never changed in my heart.)
The buildings, pocked-marked with bullet-holes
                                        from 1944,
Were Raw Umber and Mars Black, I remember.
The tablecloths were chequered the inevitable
Scarlet Lake and Titanium White.
And the sky over Berlin,
The same sky for Westerners and Easterners alike,
Was of course Cerulean Blue.
It was a Cerulean Blue day.
As for the rose which I smuggled across the border
In the pocket of my decadent Western leather
                                        jacket,
The name of that red, as I recall, was freedom.

Porto

I am walking on cobblestones
The colour of mackerel skin,
Past houses painted
Watermelon pink
And caramel yellow,
Beneath trees the colour of dried parsley
And churches the colour of clifftops.
Balconies of port red and cedar green
Project from art nouveau façades
The colour of grilled sardine flesh,
The colour of salted almonds,
The colour of the weather –
All the weather of the river,
All the weather of the sea.
Here and there a Delft blue
Cries out from the seventeenth century,
Here and there a circling gull
Cries out from an infinitely old new world.

Window on the World

I am making a window on the world,
A stained-glass window through which to look at things.
It is very much my own creation,
With reds so buoyant that they make your heart beat
                                        faster
And greens so cool that they make you taste
                                        peppermint.
The blues have the absolute assurance of first love;
The yellows, the insistence of a scarcely understood
                                        creed.
And I have purples rich with double meanings,
And oranges as straightforward as a dog.
Working in stained glass is a multi-faceted discipline:
Besides skills in design and the use of colour
You need to be able to cut glass accurately
And to solder lead so that it will hold your glass for
                                        centuries.
My window is a bold union of High Gothic and Art
                                        Nouveau,
Blending reverent formality with great swooshes of elan.
Imagine, if you will, the Virgin Mary
As she might have been depicted by Alphonse Mucha.
I would highly recommend stained glass as a medium.
It requires considerable craftsmanship
And painstaking attention to detail,
But you can always re-use the pieces
When your entire view of things
Has been shattered yet one more time.

Leaded Lights

I am gazing out
Through seventeenth-century leaded lights
At a world composed of mere suggestions:
The suggestion of a tree,
The suggestion of a house,
The suggestion of a sky.
There is not a single pane of clear glass in these
windows;
Almost every one has its own individual tint.
Watery opals and limpid greens,
Leached blues and washed-out pinks
Bespeak an age when glazed windows
Were a novel luxury of Holland's *nouveaux riches*.
Every pane has its own peculiar patterning:
Ribbed and rippled,
Fronded and faceted,
Bubbled and buckled with the weight of time,
They put four heavy centuries between me
And the briefly sunlit world outside the window.
From where I sit,
I cannot discern anything clearly through the glass:
Every element is just an indication of itself,
A possibility, the fragment of a pastel sketch
Made in preparation for a picture
That might never be painted.
What I see is not a true picture, I know;
It is not a picture at all, in fact.
But perhaps –
If I tilt my head and half-close my eyes,
If I imagine what I

(Or even someone else)
Might be seeing from this position,
Through this glass
And with this sudden flood of wintry light outside –
It is as close to a picture of the truth
As anyone might hope to see,
In this life or in any other.

Pigment

Sometimes, when the light is uncertain,
I squeeze some paint out on my palette
And simply play with it for a while,
Reminding myself that the pigment will outlive me,
Whatever I may or may not do with it.

Studio

Always the same old silence
And the same old
Always different,
Northern light.
Always the same old smell
Of dried-out clay
And dried-out paint
And dried-out ideas.
That brush I haven't touched in years.
That palette knife remains my favourite.
So many pencils sharpened in hope ...
My workbench is flecked with colours
That have not become anything at all
While ceasing to be themselves.
Here is a brownish smear
That was once Vermilion.
There is a spattering of grey
That was once Ultramarine.
And, in their tubes,
Resplendent with their unique names,
The still-virgin paints are waiting.
A Rose Madder
That is quite innocent of the world.
A Sap Green
That does not even know that it is Sap Green.
And here am I,
Surveying the debris of so many years
And reflecting on so many possibilities,
Available, as always,
Just in case an angel

Should pass through my north-facing window
And perch for one instant on my workbench,
Its wings ablaze with colours
For which only God knows the names.

Lavender

Every summer, you come back,
Like hope returning to a heart –
The hope of purity,
The hope of peace,
The hope of love.
I gently rub your flowers
Between finger and thumb
And in my little English garden
The lavender fields of Provence appear –
Cobalt Violet, Cobalt Green,
Beneath a sky of Cobalt Blue:
A carpet of heaven on earth
Which the troubadours of Occitania
Would roll up
And carry with them in their hearts
When they took their songs and lutes
And journeyed to the coldest courts of Europe
In search of purity, of peace, of love.

Apprentice and Master

All these long years, it had been there for him –
Some patch of canvas naked as the light,
Left untouched by some curious oversight,
Or just abandoned at some patron's whim;
And all the while he'd seen in every space –
As one might see it in a starry sky,
Or in a fire, or water rushing by –
The features of his own first angel's face.
So when at last the master gave him leave
To finish off a corner of one scene,
The pupil had no picture to conceive;
For in that instant, wild and serene,
The angel wings in his own heart unfurled –
His soul his brush, and in his brush the world.